Fun with Science

MINIBEASTS

ROSIE HARLOW & GARETH MORGAN

Contents

Use the symbols below to help you
identify the three kinds of practical
activities in this book.

EXPERIMENTS

GAMES

THINGS TO MAKE

Kingfisher

Introduction

In many legends beasts are ugly and frightening creatures. So what is a minibeast? Mini means small. Minibeasts are small creatures like slugs, woodlice, spiders and snails. Many of them we do not notice because they are so tiny and well hidden. Others we might find ugly and frightening. Three out of every four animals in the world are minibeasts and some of them are helpful to us in very important ways. Others can be harmful or even dangerous.

Minibeasts are invertebrates – unlike birds and fish and mammals they have no backbone. Many are insects, which have a miraculous way of changing their shape and form up to four times in their life.

Minibeasts are very adaptable. They can live on land, in water and in the air, in deserts and on mountain peaks. Wherever you live there will be minibeasts. As you carry out the experiments in the book you will learn more about the many different kinds of minibeasts living all around you.

This book covers nine main topics:
- Finding and describing minibeasts
- How minibeasts develop
- Moths and butterflies
- Minibeasts that live in water
- Predators and how animals avoid them
- Which minibeasts are helpful and which are harmful
- Social insects such as bees and wasps
- How to keep worms and look at snails
- How to help and look after minibeasts

A blue line (like the one around the edge of these two pages) indicates the start of a new topic.

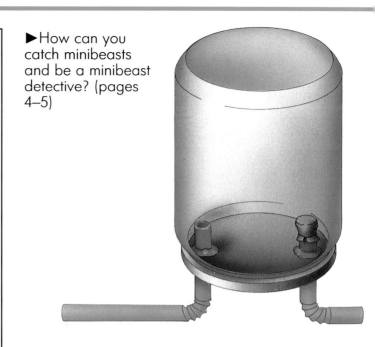

►How can you catch minibeasts and be a minibeast detective? (pages 4–5)

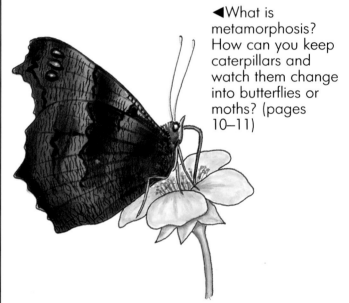

◄What is metamorphosis? How can you keep caterpillars and watch them change into butterflies or moths? (pages 10–11)

▼How can you go pond dipping and find out more about water minibeasts? (pages 16–19)

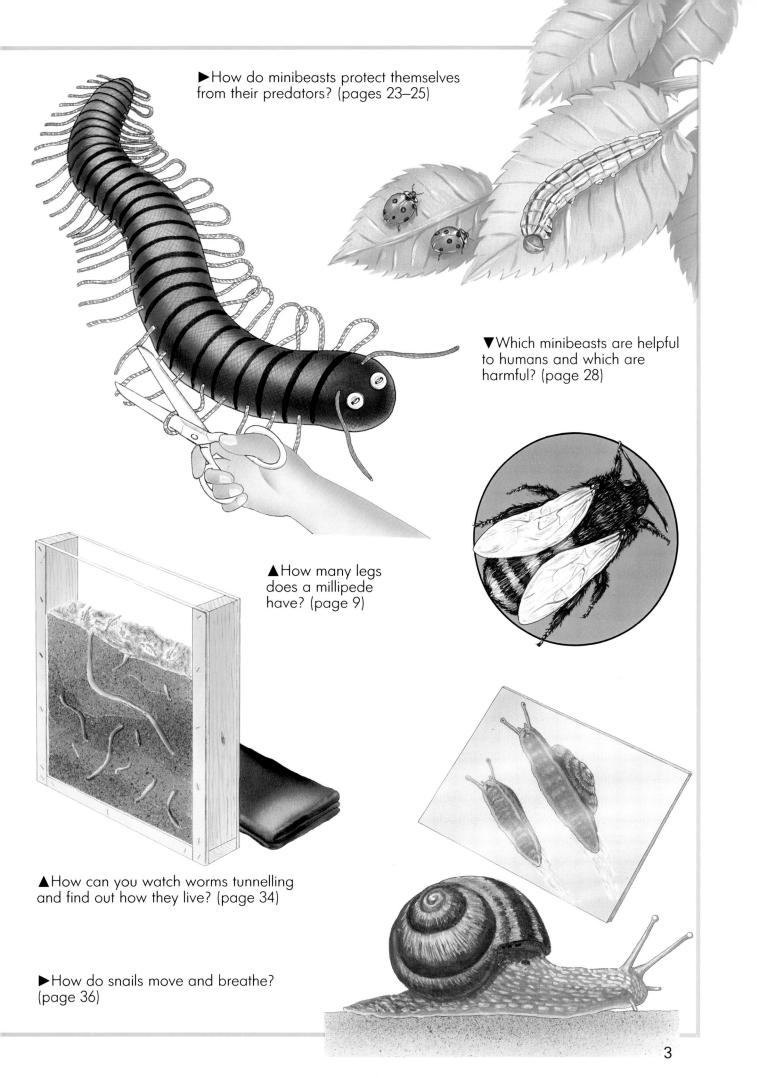

►How do minibeasts protect themselves from their predators? (pages 23–25)

▼Which minibeasts are helpful to humans and which are harmful? (page 28)

▲How many legs does a millipede have? (page 9)

▲How can you watch worms tunnelling and find out how they live? (page 34)

►How do snails move and breathe? (page 36)

Looking for Minibeasts

Minibeasts are all around us but can be hard to find as they are small and often hidden. Look in corners, cupboards, sheds and garages. Some live outside in long grass, bushes, trees or in the air or water. Many minibeasts only come out at night, so you may have to set traps for them.

Make a Pooter

A pooter is for catching minibeasts which are too small to pick up with your fingers. Find a small plastic container about 5 centimetres high and 4 centimetres across. Pierce two holes big enough to put a straw through in the lid. You need two wide, bendy straws. Put one bendy straw into each hole and seal the end with blu-tack or margarine. Tape a small piece of muslin over one of the straws to stop creatures being sucked into your mouth!

Make a Pitfall Trap

Equipment: margarine tub, stones 1–2 centimetres wide, piece of wood or cardboard, trowel.

Dig a small hole in the ground just deeper than your tub. Lay the tub in the ground and make sure the edges don't stick up. Find some stones about 2 centimetres high and put one stone at each corner. Place the wood on top to stop the rain getting in. Put some leaves and earth in the tub for the creatures to shelter in. Put in some small scraps, apple, lettuce, cheese, or tomato to attract your minibeasts.

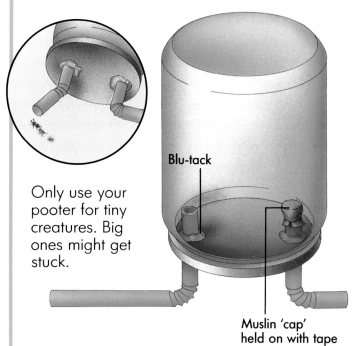

Only use your pooter for tiny creatures. Big ones might get stuck.

Blu-tack

Muslin 'cap' held on with tape

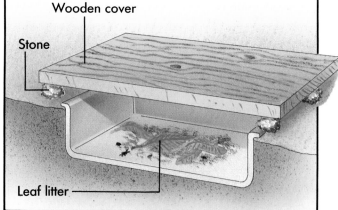

Wooden cover

Stone

Leaf litter

Be a Minibeast Detective

Using your pooter and pitfall traps try to find different minibeasts. Use a large plastic pot or tub to keep your creatures in. Remember to make your tub as similar to their natural habitat as possible. Only keep your minibeasts for one day as they will need food and proper shelter. When you have found some creatures be a minibeast detective: use these questions and a magnifier to help you find out about your minibeast. Record your findings in a notebook.

Head

Is the head large or small? Which way does it move? Does it have eyes? Where are they? Does your minibeast have **antennae** or feelers? It uses these to detect smell as we use our noses. Many minibeasts breathe through tiny holes in the sides of their body case called **spiracles**.

Wings

How many wings are there? Can you describe how it flies? (Darting, flapping, in straight line, up and down.)

Legs

How many legs does it have? Are they jointed like yours? (Your leg has a joint at the hip, the knee and the ankle.)

Where Does It Live?

Does your minibeast live in long grass, in short grass, under stones, in trees, on plants or flowers, in water, in dead wood?

Body

What colour and shape is the body? How many body parts are there? Is it **segmented** (in more than one piece)? Does the body change shape when it moves? Is it symmetrical?

Put the big creatures into the tub gently using your fingers.

Be Kind to Minibeasts

Be very careful with your minibeasts. They are very fragile. Remember you are like a giant to them!

Where Do Minibeasts Live?

People like to live in a variety of places. Some people hate the heat of the sun while other people hate the rain and the damp. Some people prefer to live alone and other people like to live in families or with friends. The next section looks at which minibeasts like to live in which places.

Habitat Survey

To find out whether minibeasts like living in different places you can do a habitat survey. A **habitat** is the place where something likes to live. A snail's habitat is a cool, damp place among leaves and soil. Take a notebook and a pencil and draw a line down the middle. In the left-hand column write the different sorts of places you can look in. Start with these: in the air, in long grass, in short grass, in trees or bushes, under stones, in water, on plants, in dead leaves, in soil, in dead wood.

Every time you find a minibeast put a tick in the right-hand column next to the place where you found it. Instead of a tick you might like to draw a tiny picture of the creature to remind yourself what it looked like. If you find new habitats add them to your list.

Try doing the survey on a warm, sunny day and then on a cloudy, damp day and see if you get different results.

Warning: When you do your habitat survey on minibeasts remember that if you lift a stone or piece of wood you are lifting the roof off a minibeast's home! Remember to put it back!

▲ Many insects and other minibeasts live in urban habitats. Flies feed off our food and can spread many diseases as they move from place to place.

Exploring Woodlice

Humans can choose where they live: in towns or the country, in dry places or damp places. These experiments show whether woodlice have favourite places to live too. Divide the tub into two halves using a thin strip of cardboard (2 centimetres high). Fill the tub with soil just over 2 centimetres high.

Sprinkle/spray a small amount of water onto the soil in one half to make it damp. Collect some woodlice and put them into the middle of the tub and see which side of the tub they prefer. Half cover a tub of fresh soil with newspapers and repeat the experiment to see if they prefer light or shade.

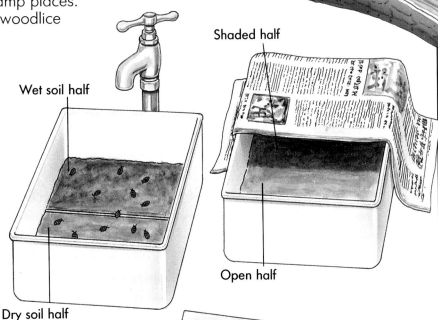

Wet soil half

Shaded half

Open half

Dry soil half

What Do Minibeasts Like Best?

Equipment: two pieces of wood, flat stone or brick.

Place the wood in a quiet corner of the garden, one piece raised 2 centimetres off the ground with stones and the other one lying flat. Make a chart as shown, drawing the creatures you find in the left-hand column. Check under the wood every day. Put one tick for each minibeast you find on the day that you find it. If you find two identical creatures put two ticks.

Your chart will help you work out which minibeasts like living alone and which in groups, and which live under tight and which under loose covers.

Tick chart

DAY	1	2	3	4
	✓✓	✓✓		
		✓✓		
		✓	✓	✓✓
		✓✓	✓✓	
	✓✓	✓✓	✓✓	✓✓
			✓✓	✓✓

Insects and You

Some minibeasts have many things in common. If you find a minibeast with three parts to its body (*see Ant Game*), six jointed legs and two antennae then it is an insect. Most insects have wings like butterflies, bees and flies. Fleas and lice do not need to fly and have no wings; they live off the blood in animals' bodies. They are called **parasites**.

Do you have anything in common with an insect? You don't look the same but you both have jointed legs and one pair of eyes. Can you think of five other things you have in common.?

Human

Your skeleton is inside your body (**endoskeleton**), while an insect has a hard outer layer (**exoskeleton**). You have warm blood, but an insect's temperature changes with the outside temperature.

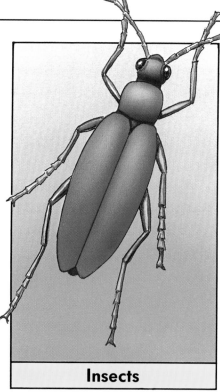

Insects

Are you the same size? Do you have antennae? What do you use to feel? Because your body is different from an insect's body you live in a different way.

The Ant Game

Equipment: plasticine, matches, dice.

If you play with a friend take it in turns to throw the dice. You must start by throwing a 1 for the head. Roll a small ball of plasticine about 1 centimetre across for the head. You must now shake a 2 for the thorax or a 6 for each antenna (you need two). Join these to the head.

Once you have the thorax you need to shake a 3 for the abdomen and a 4 for each of the legs. To make the legs you must bend a match in two places so it breaks but is still hinged.

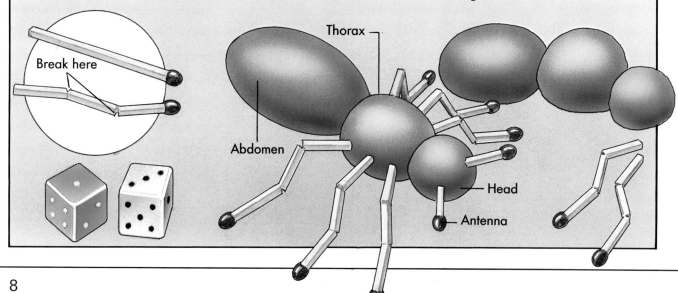

Break here

Abdomen

Thorax

Head

Antenna

Is Your Minibeast an Insect?

Go out with your collecting kit (*see page 4*) and try to find out which minibeasts are insects. Sort them into three tubs, one for insects, one for minibeasts and one for unknowns. Some insects are tricky to identify. They hide their wings by tucking them under their hard outer case. Beetles and ladybirds do this. It can also be difficult to count the number of body parts as the thorax and abdomen are often **segmented**. You may want to find a book on insects to help you.

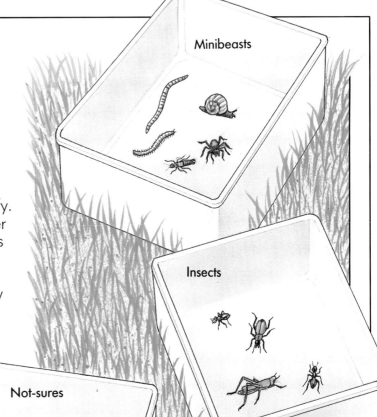

Minibeasts

Insects

Not-sures

Make a Millipede

Stuff your stocking or tight leg with filling, then sew the end up. Divide your millipede into 48 segments and thread a long piece of wool (2 metres) once through each segment. Leave a loop on each side to make the legs. Use a pipe cleaner to make two antennae.

Millipede is Latin for 1000 feet. If you count them you will see they do not really have that many.

Find a real millipede. Watch its legs ripple as it moves. The hard plates on its back are for protection and it will curl up if attacked. It can also produce a nasty smelling liquid to discourage its enemies.

Equipment: an old stocking or pair of tights. Filling: torn up newspaper or rags or stuffing. Brown wool, large-eyed needle, marker pen, pipe cleaner.

Segmented body

Woollen legs

Cut here

Metamorphosis

Humans begin life as eggs inside their mother and are born as a small version of their parents. As they grow, the bones, muscles, skin and all the parts of their body grow with them. If you had a scar on your body as a baby it would grow bigger as your body grew. Look on your shoulder for the scar from your injections as a baby.

Minibeast Metamorphosis

Some minibeasts hatch from eggs as tiny copies of their parents too. Snails, worms, and woodlice are all like this. Other minibeasts can completely change their shape and form as they grow. They begin life as an egg laid by the female. This egg hatches into a **larva**, or **caterpillar**. The larva changes into a **pupa** and the pupa changes into the adult. This process is called **metamorphosis**. Metamorphosis is a Greek word that means 'change in shape'.

Each different stage in metamorphosis performs a different function. The job of the adult is to mate and lay eggs. The job of the egg is to store information in order to grow into a new insect.

The job of the larva is to eat and grow. The pupa is a safe case inside which the larva turns into an adult.

1. Bee 2. Ant
3. Beetle 4. Butterfly

Egg

Larva

Pupa

Adult

Keeping Caterpillars

Look for eggs and caterpillars in the spring or the summer. You will find them on grasses and the leaves of plants, bushes and trees. Oak trees and nettles are good places to investigate.

You can keep the caterpillars in a container. A big sweet jar with holes in the lid or a cake tin with an acetate 'lid' are suitable. Cut a circle of acetate to make the lid and use tape to join this to the container.

Food Plants

Look for different kinds or species of caterpillar feeding on different plants. You must collect the right plant for the caterpillars to feed on or they will die. Some good ones to find are nettle, ragwort and cabbage.

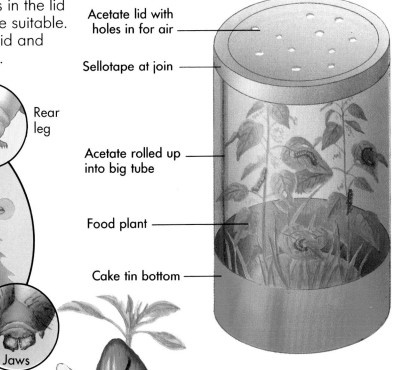

Acetate lid with holes in for air

Sellotape at join

Acetate rolled up into big tube

Food plant

Cake tin bottom

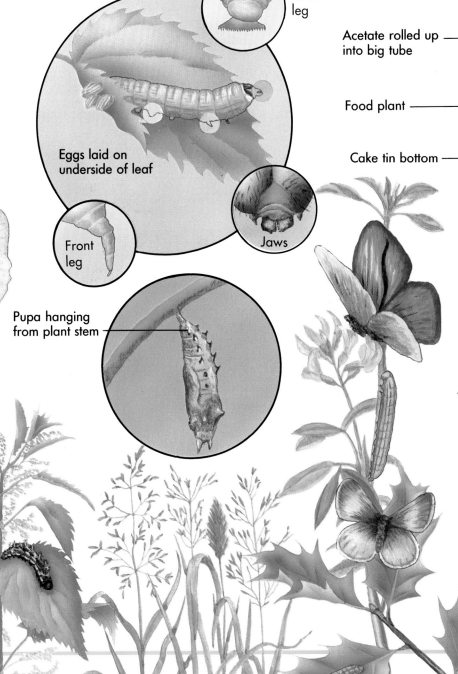

Rear leg

Eggs laid on underside of leaf

Front leg

Jaws

Pupa hanging from plant stem

Butterfly Gardening

You can attract more butterflies to your garden by planting nectar-rich shrubs and flowers. Most butterflies prefer pink, mauve or purple flowers. Buddleia, honeysuckle, lilac, cotoneaster, sweet william, marigold, cowslip and rock rose are all good. Newly born caterpillars have a soft skin which quickly hardens. As the caterpillar eats and grows the hard skin splits and the new soft-skinned caterpillar crawls out. This happens four times. Look for old skins shed by your caterpillar.

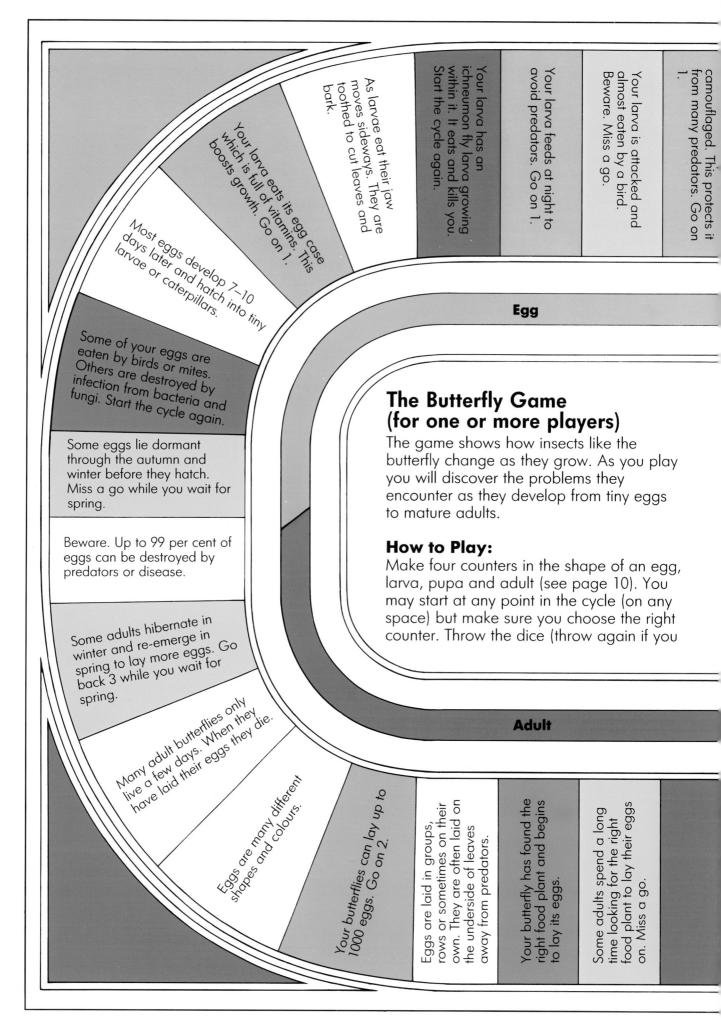

camouflaged. This protects it from many predators. Go on 1.

Your larva is attacked and almost eaten by a bird. Beware. Miss a go.

Your larva feeds at night to avoid predators. Go on 1.

Your larva has an ichneumon fly larva growing within it. It eats and kills you. Start the cycle again.

As larvae eat their jaw moves sideways. They are toothed to cut leaves and bark.

Your larva eats its egg case which is full of vitamins. This boosts growth. Go on 1.

Most eggs develop 7–10 days later and hatch into tiny larvae or caterpillars.

Egg

Some of your eggs are eaten by birds or mites. Others are destroyed by infection from bacteria and fungi. Start the cycle again.

Some eggs lie dormant through the autumn and winter before they hatch. Miss a go while you wait for spring.

Beware. Up to 99 per cent of eggs can be destroyed by predators or disease.

Some adults hibernate in winter and re-emerge in spring to lay more eggs. Go back 3 while you wait for spring.

Many adult butterflies only live a few days. When they have laid their eggs they die.

Eggs are many different shapes and colours.

The Butterfly Game (for one or more players)

The game shows how insects like the butterfly change as they grow. As you play you will discover the problems they encounter as they develop from tiny eggs to mature adults.

How to Play:

Make four counters in the shape of an egg, larva, pupa and adult (see page 10). You may start at any point in the cycle (on any space) but make sure you choose the right counter. Throw the dice (throw again if you

Adult

Your butterflies can lay up to 1000 eggs. Go on 2.

Eggs are laid in groups, rows or sometimes on their own. They are often laid on the underside of leaves away from predators.

Your butterfly has found the right food plant and begins to lay its eggs.

Some adults spend a long time looking for the right food plant to lay their eggs on. Miss a go.

Your butterfly is caught by a human and killed to be put in his collection. The cycle

As a larva grows it sheds its skin four times. The new skin is soft and allows growth to continue before it dries and becomes hard.

Some larva are brightly coloured and warn attacking birds that they are poisonous. Go on 1.

Caterpillars have many claspers with hooks to grip onto plant stems and move from leaf to leaf.

Hairs and cells on your the caterpillar's face that detect the correct food plant that detect damaged. Go back 1.

Larva

Your food plant is sprayed with insecticide. This kills your larva too. Start the cycle again.

Your larva has absorbed enough nutrients (food) and is ready to turn into a pupa.

Some larvae spin silky cocoons around their body. Others form a pupa or chrysalis, to protect them. They hang from a leaf or stem.

Some pupae are camouflaged, spined or toughened for protection. Go on 1.

Some pupae curl up in leaf litter or soil to pupate in safety.

Cells inside the pupa move about as if it in a thick 'body soup'. They rearrange themselves forming the parts of the new adult body.

get 5 or 6 as these don't count). Move clockwise. If you land on a blue space it is an advantage. If you land on a yellow space it is a disadvantage.

If you land on a pink space your creature is killed, it is the end of the cycle and you must start again. You must land exactly on all green squares. On some of these you can change your counter.,

Butterflies encounter many dangers during their short lives. You must try and complete the cycle without being killed.

Pupa

Some insects hibernate as pupae in winter and emerge in spring. Miss a go while you wait for spring.

Warm weather stimulates the adult to emerge.

Your new adult butterfly takes a few hours to dry its delicate wings. It is very vulnerable to predators. Beware. Miss a go.

The weather is warm and sunny. Butterflies are on the wing feeding on nectar from flowers.

The weather is cold and cloudy. Butterflies need sun to fly. Your butterfly is resting on a plant stem and cannot feed. Miss a go.

The warm weather returns. Adult butterflies are mating.

human and killed to be put in his collection. The cycle ends. Start again.

13

Moths and Butterflies

Both moths and butterflies are insects which start life as an egg. They then change to a caterpillar, then to a pupa and finally to an adult (*see page 10*). Because they are both insects they have many things in common. They both have three parts to their bodies, two pairs of wings, six legs and antennae.

Wings folded up while resting

Butterflies

Butterflies only fly by day. Their wings trap the Sun's warmth to give them energy to fly. Some have large 'eyes' on their wings which make the butterflies look larger than they really are which can make predators think before eating them. You can tell butterflies from moths when they are at rest. Butterflies' antennae always have knobs on the ends and butterflies hold their wings erect over their bodies when resting.

Butterflies Feeding

The caterpillar stage has powerful chewing mouthparts whilst the adult butterfly has only sucking mouthparts and lives off nectar. It uses its long proboscis to suck nectar from the base of flowers. As it does this pollen, from the stamen, sticks to its legs and is passed on to the female parts of the next flower that the butterflies visits.

Butterfly collecting Nectar

Be a Nectar Collector

Many butterflies and moths feed off nectar from flowers, and are often attracted to the flowers by their smells. Go around your garden and smell each different flower. Are the smells all the same? Can you describe them? Collect petals from the flowers you like and make a nectar cocktail.

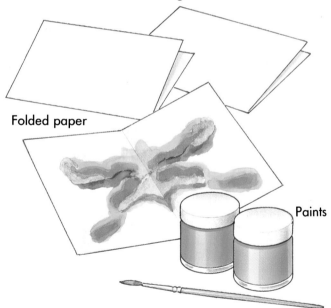

Folded paper

Paints

Symmetrical Butterfly Wings

Using a brush, put large blobs of different coloured paint onto one side of a piece of paper. Fold the clean half down onto the coloured half, smooth it with your hand, then open the paper. The image is symmetrical and can often look like butterfly wings.

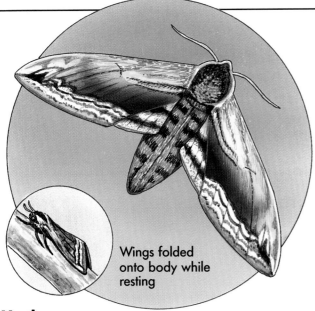

Wings folded onto body while resting

Moths

Moths get all the energy they need to fly from the food they eat. They fly, and eat, at night so do not need bright colours to attract each other. Instead the female gives off a strong smell which can attract males from a great distance. Moths usually come in dull colours which provide camouflage against their normal surroundings, making it hard for predators to find them.

Catching Moths

Moths have fragile wings, so if you catch one handle it very carefully. Put a tub with a saucer of sugar solution inside (one teaspoon sugar mixed with one tablespoon water) next to a lamp. The moths will fly towards the light, and may go to the sugar to feed.

Moths navigate using the light of the Moon, and always keep light to the same side of them when they fly. This is why they fly in circles around your lamp.

Saucer of sugar solution in box

Male moths attracted to female moths

After Dark

Wrap a piece of muslin over your tub of moths. Young female moths give off **pheromones** which a male moth can smell several kilometres away. If you attract moths to your tub then you must have some females.

15

Water Minibeasts

On this page you can find out about some of the creatures that live in water. Some spend only part of their life under water, while others live all their lives under water. Some can breathe under water using gills. Others need to come to the surface to breathe air.

Fold material over wire and sew

Poke wire into end of stick

Going Pond Dipping

To make a net, bend a piece of wire 60 centimetres long into a circle and push the ends into the cane, then tape it up. Fold the open end of one foot of the tights over the wire and sew it together.

When you go dipping take a large plastic tub to put your creatures in. Remember they need water! Don't pick them up with your hands as it is easy to squash them. Instead you can turn your net inside out into the tub and let the creatures swim off. Try dipping in different places: ponds, streams, ditches, rain tubs and even puddles are good places to investigate.

Water boatmen swim freely all around the pond. They are called boatmen because they use their legs like oars of a boat. Some eat plants and some are carnivorous. Look for those that swim on their back and others that swim on their front. They are insects and can fly.

Daphnia are very small. They swim by waving their feelers in the water and feed by filtering even tinier things from the water.

Water flea or daphnia magnified

Great diving beetle

Mosquito larva

Snails Snails eat dead plants and animals, and slime or algae growing in the water. They crawl along the bottom of ponds but can also move hanging down from the surface of the water.

A Different Life Cycle

A dragonfly spends the first two years of its life under water. Unlike a butterfly the dragonfly has only three stages in its metamorphosis (*see page 10*), egg, **nymph** and adult. It drops its eggs in the water or lays them on water plants. These hatch into tiny nymphs which are carnivorous and feed off other creatures. They have a tough outside skin which does not stretch. Eventually it splits, uncovering a new and larger skin. Dragonfly nymphs shed their skins or moult seven times before they are ready to emerge as adults (*see photo*).

Mosquito and midge larva swim by flicking and twisting suddenly in the water. They are different colours, some are red (blood worms), some are transparent. Soon they turn into pupae, which hang from the surface of the water by tiny breathing tubes.

Water skater

— Water boatman

Dragonfly nymph

Warning: Deep water is very dangerous. Do not go dipping in big rivers.

Caddis fly larva

— Pond snail

Rat-tailed maggot —

Make a Dragonfly

Use the picture to help you with the details. Blow up the balloon and tie at one end. Do not blow it up too tight as you now need to twist it twice to form the three parts of the body. Use string or tape to hold in the twisted parts. Cover the balloon with papier mâché. To make this tear up newspapers from top to bottom into strips 2–3 centimetres wide and about 20–30 centimetres long. Work on a sheet of newspaper. Paste glue onto one strip at a time, then wrap the strip onto the balloon until it is covered. Then put at least three more layers on to make it strong. Leave it to dry. When dry, paint the body. Use the photo to help you.

Make the wings from wire bent to shape and covered with muslin or tracing paper. Glue this down at the edges. Draw on the veins. Attach them using wire wrapped round the body and twisted together underneath. Use pipe cleaners or wire for the legs. Glue these to the side of the thorax. To make the eyes cut a ping-pong ball in half and glue them to the head. Paint them to look like dragonfly eyes.

Dip paper into paste

Twist and tie here

Equipment: long balloon, sticky paste (flour and water or wallpaper paste), pipe cleaners, newspaper, wire, ping-pong ball.

Pipe cleaner legs

Thin wire to make wings

Cover wings with tissue paper

Fold under and glue

Half ping-pong ball eyes

Frogs and Toads

April and May are the best times to look for frogs' or toads' spawn. Collect some and watch it change. Look in boggy areas, ditches and ponds. Only take a handful as frogs and toads are getting rare. You will need a large tank or tub with water plants to provide food and oxygen for the tadpoles (they take in oxygen from water through their **gills**). About five weeks after they have emerged they need to eat protein – cheese or bacon or natural sources of protein like mosquito larvae or other small water creatures. Watch how the legs start growing and the gills disappear at this stage. After 12 weeks the froglets are fully formed. Return them to the pond.

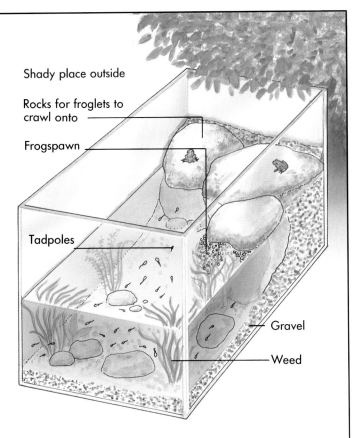

Shady place outside

Rocks for froglets to crawl onto

Frogspawn

Tadpoles

Gravel

Weed

Make a Pond

Dig a hole in the ground about 50 centimetres deep and 1 metre across, and shape it so it's narrower at the bottom. Line it with 6 centimetres of sand or newspaper then cover this with a sheet of plastic large enough to overlap the edges of the pond. Fill the pond with water then pile rocks onto the edge of the plastic sheet to keep it firm.

You can buy pond plants from garden centres or perhaps take them from another nearby pond. Stock the pond with creatures from a friend's pond or wait to see what comes to yours.

Rocks around edge

Sand

Pond plants secured in soil

Thick plastic sheet

Predators and Prey

Some minibeasts eat plants and are called **herbivores**. Some eat other creatures; they are known as **carnivores**. If a minibeast eats other minibeasts it is called a **predator**. The creature that is eaten is called the **prey**. The spider is a carnivore. It is a predator on many small insects.

Spider's Web

Spiders are able to produce a string of very fine silk from spinnerets in their abdomen. They use this silk for many purposes, though the most important is web building. The spider has developed one of the most sophisticated ways of trapping small animals. Although it looks very flimsy, one piece of silk is only 0.03 millimetres across yet is stronger than steel of the same thickness. Not all spiders make webs. Some live by catching their prey by more normal methods such as going hunting and pouncing on them unexpectedly.

Making a Spider's Web

There is more than one kind of spider's web, but the most common is the circular, or near circular type built by the garden spider. These webs are most noticeable in the autumn when they are likely to be covered in dew. Sometimes the spider sits in the centre of the web, at other times it sits beside the web, though in touch using a single silk thread, which twitches if anything disturbs the web. This type of web is never perfectly circular because the spider never finds perfectly spaced supports. The diagrams below show the major stages in building such a web. If you have a spider, give it some twigs and see how long it takes to build a web.

First the spider attaches the outer frame of the web to a convenient wall, or branch.

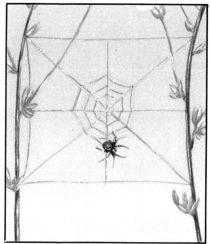

After crossing the centre with diagonals, silk is woven in spirals from the centre.

The spider reaches the outer boundary of the web. It is now complete and ready for use.

The Garden Spider Builds a Web

Stage 1. The spider lets a thread float from (1) to (2). The thread sticks when it touches a leaf or twig. The spider then joins the thread to other twigs and makes a five-sided frame.

Stage 2. The spider goes back along its first thread and makes a second loop of silk. It then drops down, leaving a 'V' shape behind. The bottom of the V makes the centre of the web. The spider spins more silk to make 'spokes' in the web.

Stage 3. The spider spins a wide spiral from the centre towards the frame.

Stage 4. The spider spins a spiral of sticky thread going from the outside to the centre. As it spins the sticky thread it eats the dry thread.

The Web Game

Making a Web

Use the pictures on page 20 to help you spin your own web. Find a forked branch of a tree with about one metre between the two branches. Make the web outside or bring a dead branch inside. Use string for the frame. Knot the string at points 1, 2, 3, 4 and 5, and back to 1 to make a five-sided frame. Cut, then tie on at point 6 and drop to 5. Cut. Cross from point 7 to 8. Cut. Make two diagonals from 1 to 3 and 2 to 4. Now work using thin sellotape as if this were your sticky silk. Work from the centre out towards the frame. Fold tape over in the centre to hold it fast. Move from the centre to the first string. Press the string hard onto the tape, spiralling outwards until you reach the frame. The sticky side of the tape should always face the same way.

'Cup' flowers

Sticky-tape web

Forked branch

Preparing the Game

First make six flowers for your branch. Cut up an egg box and stick six tissue paper petals around the cup. With a drawing pin stick flowers to the branch around the web, cups facing up. Now make ten hoverflies. Crush a small piece of tissue paper into a body shape 2 centimetres long. Wrap it in sellotape. Cut tissue paper wings and stick them onto the middle of the body.

Playing the Game

Hoverflies feed off nectar from flowers. The spider is one of their predators. Throw your hoverfly gently towards a flower in the hope that it will land there to feed. If it lands on the floor you may try again (three chances). If it does not get nectar food by then it will die of exhaustion. If it gets caught in the web you can try to free it. If you tear its wings it is dead. How long can your hoverflies survive?

Spiders Without Webs

Not all spiders make webs. Many are hunters and pounce on their prey. The wolf spider has powerful fangs, injects poison into its victim and then sucks its body dry. Because it has no web it carries its eggs in a sac underneath its body.

Catch a Web

Equipment: card, talcum powder, glue.

Spiders' webs are extremely delicate and any attempts to preserve them have to be carried out with the utmost care. Great patience and some delicacy is required. The principal difficulty is that spiders' webs are difficult to see, before and after you have preserved them.

The first thing to do is find a spider's web, preferably one hanging in an open space. So that the spider's web will be easier to see blow some talcum powder over the web. It should cover the web in a fine even layer. Next, spread a layer of glue over a piece of black card and carefully bring the card up behind the web. The object is to stick the web to the card without changing its shape, so push the card against the web very gently.

▲ A spider's web. The silk used is stronger than steel.

Cut the web around the card so that it is no longer attached to its original supports.

To preserve the web cover it with sticky-back plastic or spray it with varnish.

Money Spiders

Money spider webs are everywhere. Look in and around hedges. The web is not sticky but small creatures fall into the long strands then drop to the ground. The spiders hang in wait underneath, quickly catch their prey, then wrap them in silk for storage.

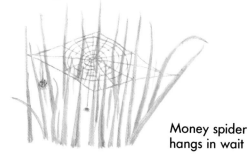

Money spider hangs in wait

Money spiders spin webs all year round but they are particularly common in the autumn. At this time of year there may be as many as one million in an area the size of half a football pitch and money spiders trap millions of insects each year.

Colour and Camouflage

All living things need some way of protecting themselves. A wasp can sting, a snail can hide in its shell, a spider can run. A caterpillar has no sting, no shell and cannot move fast, so it protects itself by **camouflaging** its body. This means its body is the same colour or shape as the things around it.

Does Camouflage Work?

Look through old magazines and cut out pictures with different colours – green, brown, red, blue, yellow, pink, orange. Cut out pieces of these colours about 3 centimetres square and stick onto cardboard. You will need about eight of each colour. For two players give half the cards to each person. Place them around the garden, in trees, on leaves and grass. Do not hide them but place them where they can be seen. Now see how many pieces you can find in five minutes. Look for your friend's pieces first and then your own. You will find that the most difficult to see are those that match the background colour most closely. There are five camouflaged minibeasts hidden in the picture above. See if you can spot them.

Disguise a Caddis

A caddis fly spends most of its year-long life under water as a larva. To protect itself the larva builds a camouflaged case around its body. Make a caddis case using a thin cardboard tube. Close the tube at one end with tape and cover it all with glue. Cover your case with natural materials. Make your caddis from plasticine and put it in the case.

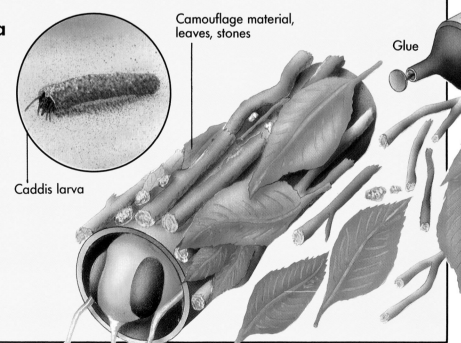

Caddis larva

Camouflage material, leaves, stones

Glue

Means of Protection

Different minibeasts have different ways of protecting themselves. This illustration shows you some examples of minibeasts that hide, or sting, or run away. On your next minibeast hunt, check to see how many you can find.

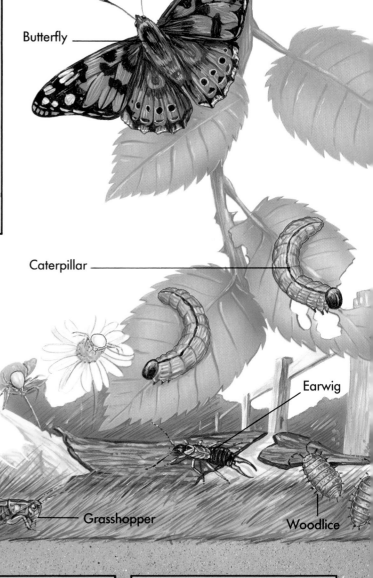

Butterfly

Caterpillar

Earwig

Millipede

Grasshopper

Woodlice

Minibeast Enemies

The most common enemies of minibeasts are lizards, mice and birds. Both moles and badgers eat mostly worms and when other food is hard to find foxes and badgers will often eat beetles. Guess which animals might eat the different minibeasts in this picture.

Snails and Slugs
Snails have a shell and can retreat or hide in it to protect themselves. Slugs are covered in mucous which makes it difficult for birds to pick them up.

Caterpillars
Many caterpillars camouflage themselves to hide from predators. Others have bright colours and patterns to warn the birds that they are poisonous.

Crickets and Grasshoppers
Grasshoppers and crickets protect themselves using camouflage. They can also jump very suddenly to escape danger. They can jump up to 1 metre high, which is 40 times their height.

Worms

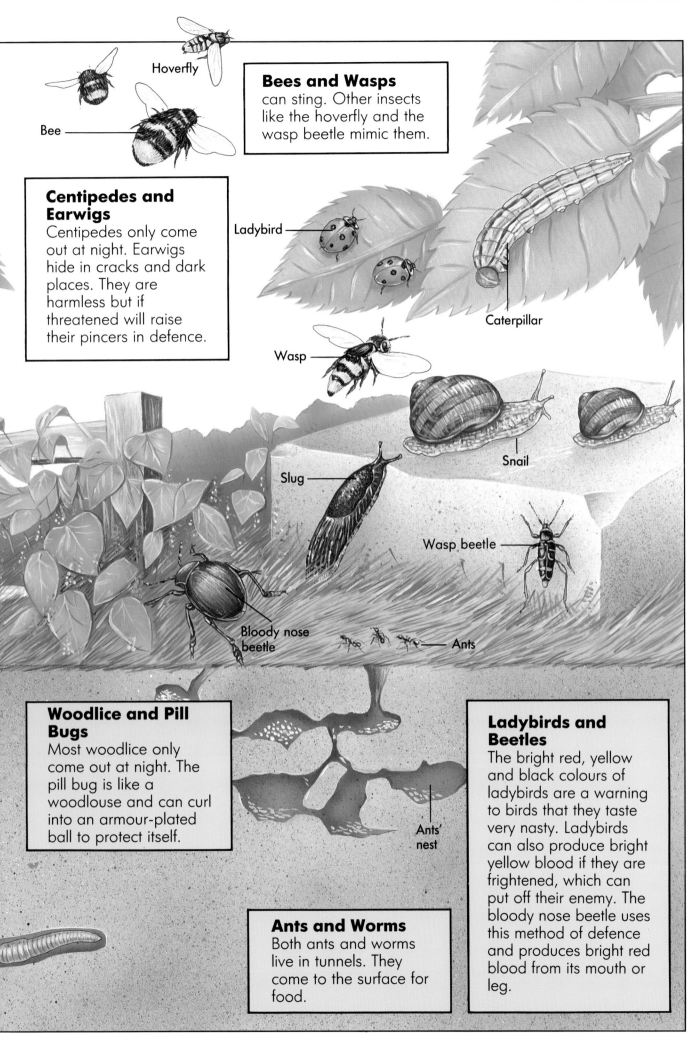

Hoverfly

Bee

Bees and Wasps
can sting. Other insects like the hoverfly and the wasp beetle mimic them.

Centipedes and Earwigs
Centipedes only come out at night. Earwigs hide in cracks and dark places. They are harmless but if threatened will raise their pincers in defence.

Ladybird

Caterpillar

Wasp

Snail

Slug

Wasp beetle

Bloody nose beetle

Ants

Ants' nest

Woodlice and Pill Bugs
Most woodlice only come out at night. The pill bug is like a woodlouse and can curl into an armour-plated ball to protect itself.

Ladybirds and Beetles
The bright red, yellow and black colours of ladybirds are a warning to birds that they taste very nasty. Ladybirds can also produce bright yellow blood if they are frightened, which can put off their enemy. The bloody nose beetle uses this method of defence and produces bright red blood from its mouth or leg.

Ants and Worms
Both ants and worms live in tunnels. They come to the surface for food.

Watch that Warning (Game)

Cut out ten circles of paper about 5 centimetres across. Colour five with warning colours and patterns and the other five with camouflage colours and patterns. Use the creatures illustrated here and on pages 24 and 25 to help you. Tape a peppercorn to the back of the warning cards and a jelly baby to the back of the camouflage cards. Spread the ten cards on the grass, colour facing up. Each card is a juicy minibeast. Tell your friend to be a hungry bird. They must choose which ones to eat without knowing what is on the back. When they have chosen one they must bite into and taste the food on the back. See how long it takes them to learn which minibeasts taste good and which taste bad.

Use of Colours

For various reasons insects are many different colours. Some use their colours to hide, others to show up more clearly. The bright, coloured ones use colour and pattern to recognise each other. The insects above use colour to warn predators that they are poisonous.

Make a Giant Ladybird

Equipment: Newspaper, paste, balloon, paint.

Cover a round balloon with papier mâché (see page. 18). Leave it to dry overnight and then cut the balloon shape in half. Mark on your ladybird's head, thorax and wing cases and then paint its bright warning colours. Use one of the pictures to help you. Sellotape on some pipe cleaner legs. You can use the other half of your balloon to make a beetle or woodlouse. Using the same method and different shaped balloons you can make all sorts of model minibeasts.

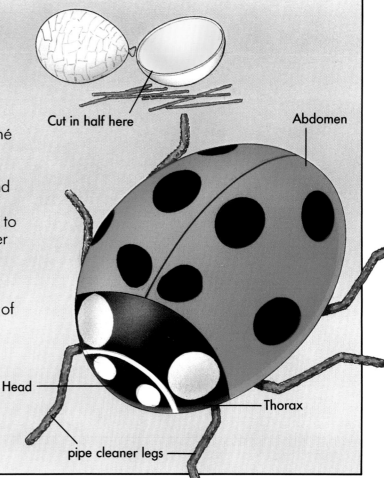

Cut in half here

Abdomen

Head

Thorax

pipe cleaner legs

Play the Ladybird Game

Equipment: card, eggbox, raisins, dice, paint.

Cut a square of card 15 × 15 cm. Cover with leaves. This is the board for the game and is the garden in which the minibeasts live. Paint the cups from the eggbox red with black spots. This game shows that the number of ladybirds depends on the number of aphids in the summer. One raisin = 1000 aphids.

To play: 1. Throw the dice for April. If you throw 3, put out three raisins and begin to feed one ladybird. Each ladybird needs 1000 aphids per month to survive. 2. Roll dice for May. Feed the ladybird. 3. If you have some good months you can begin to feed other ladybirds, so when you have earned five raisins spare start feeding more ladybirds. Keep feeding all the ladybirds until September. Was it a good year for the ladybirds? Playing this game shows that during years with plenty of aphids, many ladybirds survive.

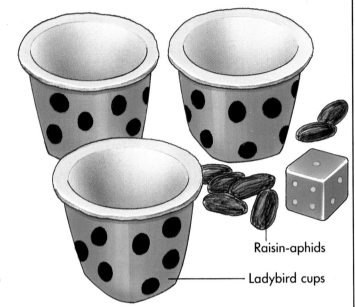

Raisin-aphids

Ladybird cups

Make a Creepy Crawly Course

Imagine you are the size of a ladybird or ant. What would the world look like? Use a magnifying glass to find out, or a cardboard tube which makes everything bigger when you look down it. Go into the garden and crawl around looking very closely at the magic world of minibeasts. Set up a miniature assault course. Use sticks, leaves and stones to build your course, and perhaps try using a saucer of water.

Did you know Ladybird larvae are unable to sense their prey until they touch it. If they find aphids they will eat up to 15 in one day.

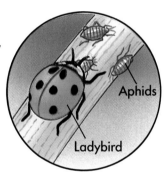

Aphids

Ladybird

Ladybird, ladybird fly away home,
Your house is on fire, your children will burn . . .

Some people think this is a warning to ladybirds because in September farmers used to burn the hop fields which were full of ladybirds.

Sticks

String tied to sticks

Helpful or Harmful?

Some minibeasts are helpful to humans, some are really harmful and some are just a nuisance. Ants are a nuisance, as are the larvae of the woodworm beetles that make holes in furniture until it falls apart. In Africa swarms of locusts eat everything in their path and can strip a field of crops in a few hours. Mosquitoes, fleas and other insects carry diseases like malaria.

▲ Many insects, such as this butterfly, feed from nectar in flowers. This is helpful to humans as it fertilizes the flower and makes the seeds grow.

Why Do Insects Visit Flowers?

Insects go to flowers looking for nectar. They are attracted to the flower by the bright colours and the smell or scent. Do an experiment to find out which scents and colours attract which insects.

Colour Make cards and paint them different colours. Each card should be about 30 centimetres square, yellow, red, blue, green, pink, orange or black. Lay the card squares on the grass on a warm sunny day. Find out which is the most popular colour by keeping a record of the insects that visit the cards.

Scent Insects are also attracted by scent and the knowledge that food or nectar is near.

Pick the least visited colours and add a smear of honey. Insects will now visit these colours, attracted by the smell.

Keeping records on a clipboard

	moth	bee	wasp	fly
Red	✓✓	✓		
Blue				
Yellow			✓	✓
Green		✓✓		✓
Purple	✓✓		✓	✓
			✓	

Coloured card

Social Insects

Bees, wasps and ants live in colonies so can help look after each other. Some collect food, some look after young, some mate and lay eggs.

A colony of bees has about 50,000 workers, 300 males and one queen. The males' job is to try and mate with the queen who flies high into the sky, where only the strongest male can follow and mate with her. The queen's job is to lay eggs, as many as 2000 in a day.

It's a Bee's Life

Worker bee

The workers' job is to feed the growing larvae. This keeps them very busy as each larva needs about 1300 meals a day! For the first three days the workers feed them on royal jelly (a mixture of honey, pollen and a special juice from their glands). After this, if they are fed only on royal jelly they become new queens, but if their diet changes to a mixture of honey and pollen they become workers.

▲ Worker bees feeding the growing larvae. Each hexagon is a cell containing one bee larva.

When a new queen is born the old queen leaves, taking about half the colony with her. This is called swarming.
If two new queens emerge at the same time they will fight to the death. The winner will kill all other queen larvae or pupae so as to have no rivals. During the winter bees feed on honey stored in the hive but if it is cold many will die.

Worker Bee Experiment

Worker bees can carry up to half their body weight in nectar and sometimes travel 10–13 kilometres to a good patch of flowers. Weigh yourself and calculate half your body weight. Find something of that weight and try carrying it. Could you go 13 kilometres?

Workers also have to build up the winter's supply of honey. To make 500 grams of honey, bees fly 80–160 thousand kilometres. It is hardly surprising that many die of exhaustion, and it is estimated that up to 1500 die each day in a typical colony.

Travelling with a heavy load

Busy as a Bee

Your finger is the bee. Cut out wings to stick on your finger and mark stripes on the body with a felt tip pen. Visit the most brightly coloured and sweetly scented flowers you can find. Put your finger in towards the nectar at the base of the flower. Your bee is trying to feed on nectar. Go to another flower and look for more, this transports pollen which fertilises the plants. Without insects many of our food plants (fruits, vegetables, etc.) would not be fertilised.

Choose a Flower

Find a flower that is visited often by bees. Choose one bud and tie a woollen marker on it so you can find it again. For ten minutes each day watch the flower and note down how many insects visit it. There should be a day when pollen ripens and gives off the most scent and many more bees visit. Remember that on cloudy days insects are less active.

Plastic wings

Striped finger bee

Bees collecting pollen and nectar

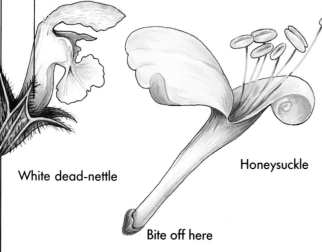

Nectar stored here

White dead-nettle

Honeysuckle

Bite off here

Taste the Nectar

It is possible to taste nectar from some flowers – easy ones to try are honeysuckle and white dead-nettle. Look for a flower that is fully opened. Pull gently from the plant, bite off 1 millimetre at the end and suck.

Did you know? A worker bee has a barbed sting at the end of its abdomen. If it uses its sting it will die as the tip of its abdomen is ripped out. The male bees or drones can't sting, but beware! The queen bee can sting repeatedly.

Bumble Bees

Look for bumble bees. They are thicker and more hairy than honey bees. They live in colonies of about 150 bees. In autumn they all die except the new queens.

Making Bee Homes

Many of the bees and wasps we see are not from colonies like honey bees or bumble bees. They live on their own, making small nests in soil or hollowstems and holes. The female lays a few eggs in each hole and leaves a stock of pollen and nectar as food for the new larvae. She then dies and the new bees appear the following spring.

Make some homes for solitary bees and wasps. Plug one end of each straw with plasticine or cotton wool. Put them in a tin can or attach them under a window sill in a warm sunny place.

Use strong tape or wire to attach the bunches of straws to the windowsill.

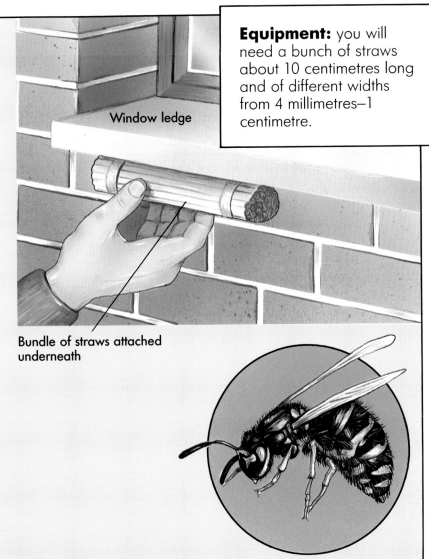

Window ledge

Bundle of straws attached underneath

Equipment: you will need a bunch of straws about 10 centimetres long and of different widths from 4 millimetres–1 centimetre.

Wasps

Wasps also live in social colonies like bees. There are usually about 2000 wasps in each colony. In spring wasps are busy collecting food for their hungry larvae. They use their sting to kill small insects like aphids and caterpillars. The larvae produce a sweet saliva that feeds the wasps until they are all hatched in late summer. Then they look for food in other places — rotting fruit or jam . Wasps are a nuisance and can be very dangerous if they sting you in the mouth or throat. The photo on the right shows a wasps' nest.

Life In the Ant Colony

Ants are social insects like bees and wasps. The different members of their colony have different jobs to do. First the queen rubs off bits of her wings, as she will not need them again. She then tunnels into the ground and makes a chamber where she will lay her eggs. The males' job is to mate with the queen. She raises the first worker larvae on her own. Once they have emerged, some nine months later, they will begin to run the colony for her. Workers have different jobs:

Remember: ants can sting.

some are nurses tending the young, some are cleaners, and some forage for food. The foragers feed the other workers, by passing liquid food directly into their mouths. As they do this they rear up on their legs and look as though they are kissing. This is also the way the queen passes messages to the ants in her colony. She secretes liquid 'messages' on her body that the workers lick off her and pass around the colony. They tell the ants what needs doing in the colony.

Make a Formicarium

Equipment: two sheets of perspex 25 centimetres square, one sheet 5 × 25 centimetres, three wooden battens 5 × 25 centimetres and 15 millimetres thick, screws, tape.

Screw the perspex sheets to the wooden battens as shown and attach the lid using strong tape. Make sure they fit tightly to prevent the ants escaping. Look for black ants to fill the formicarium under garden paths and flat stones or yellow ants in grassy mounds. When you find the nest dig down to try and find the queen, who is much bigger than the workers. Put as many workers as possible into the formicarium with the queen. Gently fill the formicarium with enough soft earth to cover the ants, so fill it about three-quarters full. Place some of the following food in with them: ripe fruit, seeds and small scraps of cheese or jam. Occasionally spray the soil with water to give the ants something to drink.

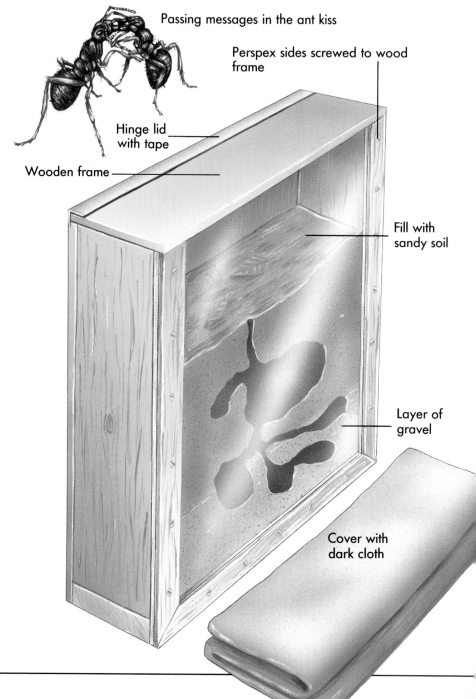

Passing messages in the ant kiss

Perspex sides screwed to wood frame

Hinge lid with tape

Wooden frame

Fill with sandy soil

Layer of gravel

Cover with dark cloth

Ant Safari

You may be able to find ant colonies thriving in the garden. A favourite place for ants to make a nest is under a large flat stone. Look under slabs in your garden. If you have any old bricks or slabs lay them out in a deserted corner of the garden and see if you can encourage an ant colony to nest there. Putting out attractive food might help. Look for ants in different stages of their life cycle. The eggs are small and white, the larvae are white maggots and the pupae are like tiny beans.

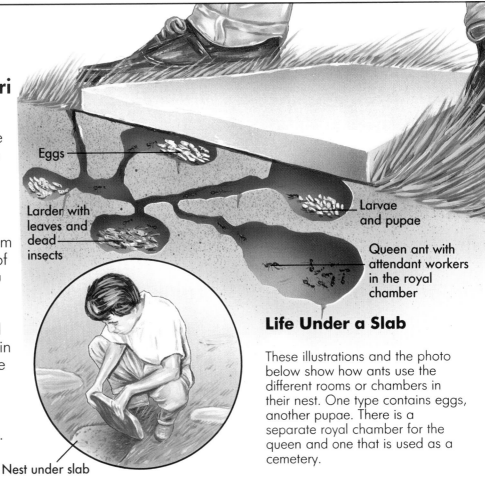

Eggs

Larder with leaves and dead insects

Larvae and pupae

Queen ant with attendant workers in the royal chamber

Nest under slab

Life Under a Slab

These illustrations and the photo below show how ants use the different rooms or chambers in their nest. One type contains eggs, another pupae. There is a separate royal chamber for the queen and one that is used as a cemetery.

How Worms Help

Worms tunnel beneath the soil. Their tunnels can reach a depth of 1.5 metres. Worms eat their way through the soil in search of dead plant material. The matter that passes through them is pushed towards the surface where it forms worm casts. With two million worms living in an area the size of a football pitch a huge amount of earth can be shifted.

Worm Dances

Worms usually only come to the surface at night when they are not in danger of being eaten. Some birds have a way of tricking them to the surface by tapping or pecking at the ground. If the soil is damp you can entice them to the surface by doing a worm dance: gently stamp your feet, making sure you don't keep moving them or you might tread on the worms. Continue for about five minutes or until worms start popping up.

Make a Wormery

Make your wormery the same as the formicarium (see page. 32). Put in different layers of stones and soil, with 5 centimetres gravel at the bottom. Put in two or three layers of different coloured, moist, soil. The different layers will enable you to see how worms help to move soil about. Make sure you keep a layer of leaves or grass cuttings on the surface. Watch how they pull these down into the burrows. Both ends of a worm look similar, but on closer inspection you will see that one end, the head, is more pointed than the other.

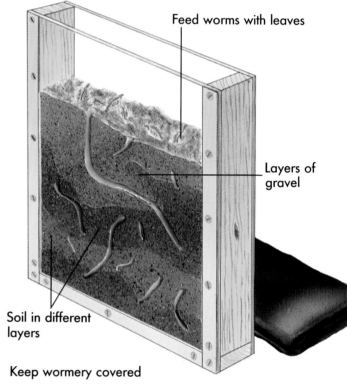

Feed worms with leaves

Layers of gravel

Soil in different layers

Keep wormery covered

You may see some worms with a thick band around the middle of their body. This is where they store their eggs. The belt or saddle gradually moves down the body and eventually drops off, forming a protective **cocoon** around the eggs.

Muscular segments stretch and contract

Saddle, contains eggs

Bristles

Worm Experiments

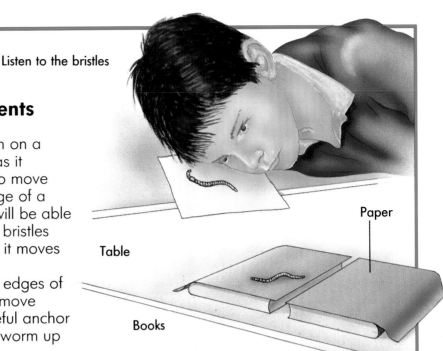

Paper

Table

Books

Listening to worms: Put a worm on a piece of moist paper and watch it as it contracts and spreads its muscles to move forward. Hold the paper on the edge of a table and put your ear close. You will be able to hear the scratching sound of the bristles underneath its body that grip when it moves along.

These bristles grip the soil on the edges of the burrows and help the worm to move forward. They can also make a useful anchor if a hungry bird is trying to pull the worm up out of the ground.

Bridging the gap: Put two books on the table. lay a sheet of paper on each but leave a gap of 3 centimetres between the two sheets. Sprinkle water on one sheet so it is damp. Put your worm on the dry sheet and watch it 'bridge the gap' to get to the wet sheet.

This shows that worms prefer damp places, so you should always keep the soil in your wormery damp.

Other Worms

There are many millions of earthworms constantly tunnelling beneath the soil. There are also many types of earthworm, of varying sizes, which live in a wide range of habitats some preferring rotting material like compost, for example the red and orange brandling worm. There are also many types of smaller worm which are not the same family as earthworms and are normally too small to find with the naked eye.

Worm Watching

Measure out 1 square metre on an open piece of grass. If you can find an area with worm casts so much the better, as this is a sign that worms are already active. Pin down some different worm foods under a piece of fine netting (old net curtain works well). Try different leaves and small bits of fruit or vegetable. Make a map, marking where you have put everything. Come back each morning to see if anything has gone.

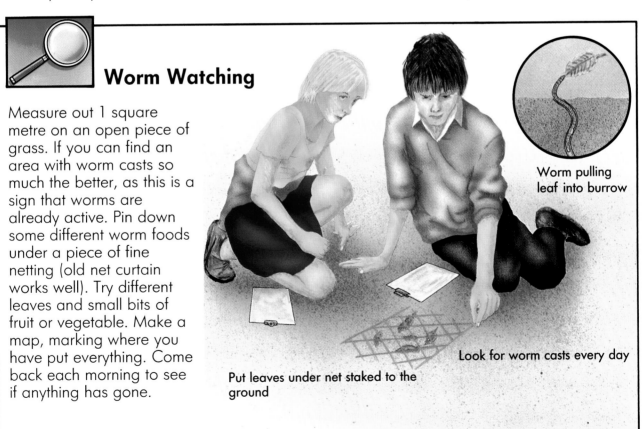

Worm pulling leaf into burrow

Put leaves under net staked to the ground

Look for worm casts every day

Snail Watching

Snails try to avoid hungry predators by only coming out at night. This also stops them drying up in the sun. If it is too hot or too cold the snail can shut its door and seal the entrance to its shell with a layer of hard mucous.

Most snails eat plants but some are carnivores and eat other small creatures. Snails are **hermaphrodite**. This means they have both male and female parts to their body. When mating the snails stick together and shoot a 'love dart' carrying sperm into the other snail. They can then both lay eggs.

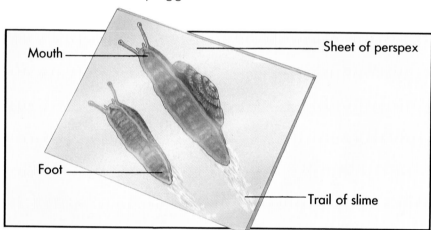

Shell
Feelers or antennae
Breathing hole
Foot

Put your snail on a sheet of stiff clear plastic. Wait till it has come out of its shell and started exploring. Turn the plastic upside down and watch the rippling muscles of the snail's foot as it moves along. A snail leaves a trail of slime as it moves. This is important to help it to slide over rough or sharp objects.

Mouth
Sheet of perspex
Foot
Trail of slime

Garden snail
Edible snail
White-lipped snail

Anvil stone   Broken shells

Do Snails Have a Home?

A snail carries its home, its shell, on its back. Leave an old flower pot or margarine tub on its side in a damp place in the leafy undergrowth. Check daily to see if snails visit. If you get a visitor paint a red spot on its shell and see if it returns.

Different Shells

A snail's shell is very important. It stops the soft body from drying out. If it is very hot in summer or cold in winter the snail can seal the entrance of the shell with a layer of hard mucous. As the snail grows the shell is enlarged from the entrance.

Snail Snacks

Snails make a tasty meal for any bird that can open their shell. The song thrush is very good at this. It bashes the snail against a hard stone to crack the shell. Around where this has happened you will find pieces of broken snail shells.

Developing Multi-storey Minibeast Homes

Find a quiet corner of a garden where you can make your own minibeast housing development. You will need to let the grass and wild flowers grow so check that this is all right with whoever looks after the garden. Use all the ideas in this book to help you provide homes for as many creatures as possible. To encourage butterflies to the top storey of your high open-air garden let the grass and nettles grow and plant some wild flowers (*see page 11*). To encourage basement tenants leave some bricks and slabs about. Pile some old bricks, flower pots and bits of wood or piping to provide hidden nooks and crannies for those that live on middle storeys. Put out bits of food like vegetables, leaves and pieces of fruit to encourage ground floor dwellers. An old rotting log is an excellent addition, providing secluded rooms and facilities for many species. An old flat bowl dug into the ground and filled with water encourages those creatures that prefer to spend their time under water. Caring developers will check regularly that their tenants are happy and that facilities are maintained to standard.

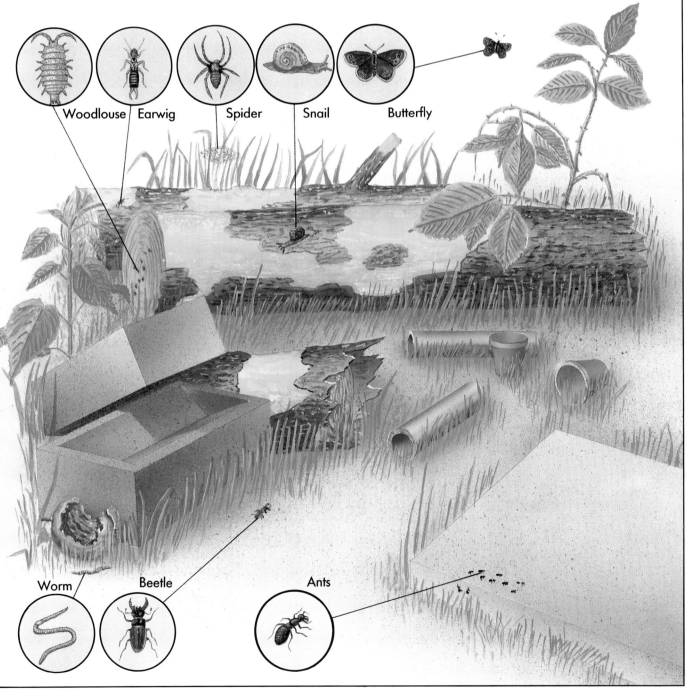

Woodlouse   Earwig   Spider   Snail   Butterfly

Worm   Beetle   Ants

Make a Minibeast Meadow Frieze

Equipment: grasses, plants, paints, white wax crayon, large sheet of white paper.

To make the background to your meadow draw lots of thick vertical lines like grass shadows down the page. Mix up a watery pale green or blue paint and brush this over the wax. The thin paint will not colour the waxed areas.

Paint one side of your grasses and plants, then press them gently against your meadow picture to make a print. Cut out and stick on bright coloured tissue paper shapes to make flowers. Your meadow is now ready to be filled with minibeasts. Make careful drawings by sketching outside from real life. Sometimes if you look on window ledges, you can find dead minibeasts, as well.

A Mini-Visitors' Book

Many people keep visitors' books and record the dates and activities of their visiting guests. Record the visits you get from minibeasts where you live. Make one book for inside guests and one for outside guests. Record what they do on their visits, the date when they arrive, and the date they leave.

Prints of grasses and flowers in the meadow

Helping Out

Minibeasts are useful to us in many ways. There is an enormous amount of matter locked in the chemical structure of all living things. When they die this can be released and returned to the earth and used again by plants to make more sugars. Minibeasts contribute to this by feeding off the remains of dead animals and breaking down the materials within. Smaller micro organisms such as bacteria further this process and return much of the chemicals in dead organic matter to the soil.

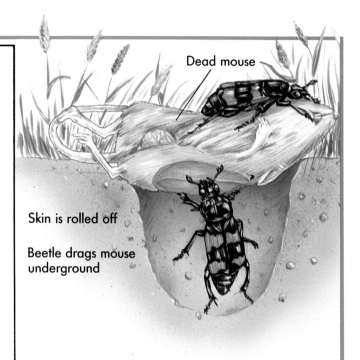

Dead mouse

Skin is rolled off

Beetle drags mouse underground

Sexton Beetles

These are some of the larger beetles that help recycle dead animals and plants. The beetle digs a hole under the carcass, and then pulls it into the hole. As this happens the skin is rolled off the body. Eggs are laid in the hole and the flesh provides food for the larvae.

Dor beetle making dung ball

Dor Beetle

The dor beetle is also called a dung beetle. It digs a burrow up to 60 centimetres deep and buries a ball of dung there for its larvae to eat. This helps to fertilise the soil.

Vital Cleaners

Place a small dead animal or bird in a plastic container or margarine tub with holes pierced in it. Fill the container with soil, seal with a lid and bury it 20 centimetres under the ground. Mark the spot where you buried it. Dig it up four weeks later. The fleshy parts of your creature will have been consumed by mini- and micro-beasts in the soil. Extract the skeleton carefully and you may be able to reassemble it.

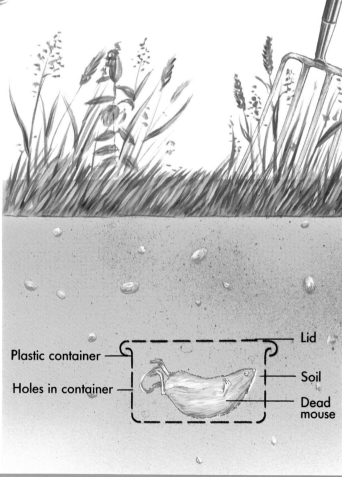

Plastic container

Holes in container

Lid

Soil

Dead mouse

Index

Editors: Thomas Keegan and Annabel Warburg
Designer: Ben White
Illustrators: Kuo Kang Chen • Oxford Illustrators

Cover Design: Terry Woodley
Picture Research: Elaine Willis

The authors would like to thank their colleagues from the South Oxfordshire Countryside Education Trust, especially Jacquie Fynn, and the many others who have helped with ideas for this book.

Photographic Acknowledgements

The publishers wish to thank the following for supplying photographs for this book:

Page 6 Heather Angel/Biofotos; 17 Nature Photographers; 18 Nature Photographers; 22 NHPA/N.R. Coulton; 28 Nature Photographers; 29 NHPA/Stephen Dalton; 31 Swift Picture Library; 33 NHPA/G.B. Bernard.

KINGFISHER
An imprint of Larousse plc
Elsley House, 24–30 Great Titchfield Street,
London W1P 7AD

This reformatted edition published by Kingfisher 1997
10 9 8 7 6 5 4 3 2 1
Originally published by Kingfisher 1991
© Grisewood and Dempsey Ltd. 1991

A CIP catalogue record for this book is available from the British Library.

ISBN 1 85697 373 5

Phototypeset by Wyvern Typesetting Ltd, Bristol
Printed by South China Printing Company H.K.